Learn to Sew: Kids

My First
Sewing Machine Book

Learn to Sew: Kids

My First

Sewing Machine Book

Alison McNicol

Learn to sew and make *cool* stuff!

A Kyle Craig Publication

www.kyle-craig.com

First published in 2010 by Kyle Craig Publishing

Text and illustration copyright © 2010 Alison McNicol

Design and illustration: Julie Anson

Contents

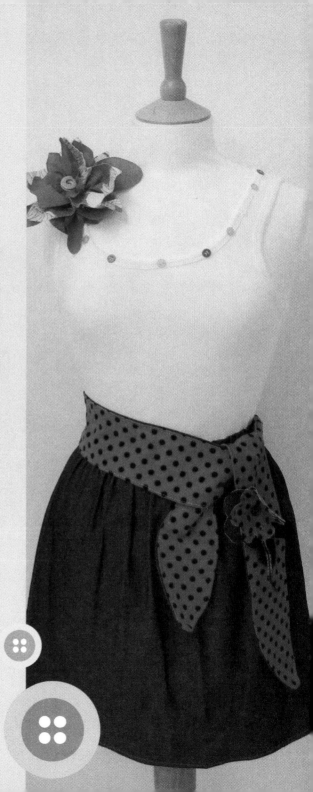

Alison and some of her pupils

Hi there!

I shall never forget my first ever sewing machine, given to me by Father Christmas when I was 7 or 8 years old! It started my love of sewing and making things, and now I just LOVE to help others discover how much fun sewing can be!

Are you ready to start learning to use a sewing machine? Perhaps you've just been given your very own machine, or someone is allowing you to use theirs? How exciting!

Using a sewing machine is pretty easy once you know how. Just take your time to learn all about your machine and what each part does, and always pay close attention when you're using the machine to make sure you sew safely.

This book is super easy to follow and soon you'll be ready to make some very cool projects too!

Sew...what are you waiting for? Let's SEW!

Alison McNicol

Sewing kit essentials

It's a good idea to get yourself a good sewing box to keep your kit all in one place. This could be anything from a classic wooden workbox, to a fancy sewing box or even an old cookie tin. The items listed here are the basic items you should need to get going. Once you get the sewing bug there are all sorts of other bits and bobs you can add to your collection!

Dressmakers Chalk: This is also called *tailors chalk* and comes in different shapes, such as pencils, triangles or circles. It's is used for drawing lines on fabrics. Use white chalk for dark fabrics and coloured chalk for light or patterned fabrics.

Needles: It's handy to have a few different sized hand sewing needles. A medium size needle will do for most jobs, but a tough fabric like denim will need a thicker needle. A needle with a big 'eye' is needed for thicker thread or embroidery thread.

Pins: Dressmaking pins can come as basic steel pins or with a variety of colourful heads. A pincushion is also handy for storing pins while you work.

Seam Ripper: This is also called an *unpicker*. It has a sharp little hook that helps you to easily rip out seams or tacking. Very handy if you make a mistake on the sewing machine!

Sewing Machine Needles: The needlesize and type is determined by the fabric you are using. The needles your machine comes with will be fine for most standard fabrics or cottons. For other fabrics, such as denim, silk or stretchy fabrics you will need to use special needles that are the correct size for the fabric.

Tape Measure: A tape measure is essential for measuring fabrics and taking measurements. But you can also use a ruler or solid measuring stick.

Scissors: It's a good idea to have a few pairs for different purposes:
    Dressmaking scissors: have long, sharp steel blades and are for cutting out fabric pieces.
    Paper scissors: useful for cutting out paper patterns so you do not blunt your dressmaking scissors.
    Pinking Shears: cut a zig zag edge which can stop fabric from fraying.
    Sewing scissors: smaller than dressmaking scissors and are handy for trimming seams or threads.

Fabrics & threads

The choice of fabric is important when planning a project. As well as looking at the colour and pattern of a fabric, think about how it will look as the finished item. Is it heavy enough for the purpose, will it hang well when sewn and not crease too much?

There are so many cool fabrics available, and it's great to start a collection so you will always have some fabric to hand whenever you feel like making something!

Fabrics

Calico: is a plain natural coloured woven cotton that has a gorgeous old fashioned feel to it and comes in a variety of widths.

Cotton: one of the most versatile and popular fabrics, cotton is a natural fabric made from the hairs that cover the seed podof the cotton plant. Available in a variety of light to medium weights.

Man made fabrics: these include polyester, nylon and rayon. Some of these are slippery and crease easily, while others likepolyester are very crease-resistant. You can also get a mix of man-made and natural fabrics, like poly cotton, that combines the best qualities of both fabrics.

Threads

Cotton Thread: cotton thread is a fine, mercerised thread that is used for hand and machine stitching, usually on natural fabrics such as cotton, linen and woollen fabric.

Polyester Thread: this is a popular multi-purpose type of thread that can be used on all types of fabrics, for hand and machine stitching, and comes in a wide range of colours.

Silk Thread: this is a fine, yet strong thread that can be used for both hand and machine stitching. It is commonly used on silk and wool fabrics, and for hand-stitched buttonholes on finer fabrics.

How to use...
Fabric

So that we can follow **PROJECTS** cards and **PATTERNS**, it's important to know what all the words mean. With fabric, we talk about the **right** side and the **wrong** side of the fabric.

STEP 1

The *right side*, is the nice side, the one you want to be seen.

 The *wrong side* is the back of the fabric or the nasty side. With patterned fabric it's usually quite easy to see which side is which.

STEP 2

If we're sewing something with straight or blanket stitch that we want to be seen, we may be told to place the *wrong sides* together. We then sew our stitches where needed.

STEP 3

If we're sewing something where we don't want the stitches to be seen — like a pillow or clothes — we may be told to put the *right sides* together before sewing.

STEP 4

Now when we turn it inside out — the *right side* is on the *outside*! See?

How to use...
A sewing machine

SEW...now you're ready to use a sewing machine?!

Learning to use a sewing machine is a bit like learning to drive a car or fly an aeroplane — we must learn how it all works first before we can use it **SAFELY**!

FIRST we're going to learn what all the **parts are called**, and what they **do**. We'll also learn some important things about sewing machine **safety** too.

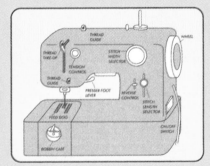

THEN, we're going to learn how to **thread** our machines properly. Without thread, we wouldn't be able to make any stitches!

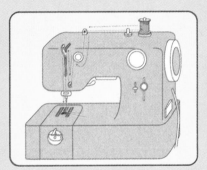

NEXT we'll see how to how to **control** our fabric as it passes through the machine so we make stitches exactly where we want them.

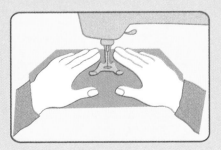

LASTLY we'll practice using the machine to sew **straight lines**, **curves** and **turn corners**.

They say Practice Makes Perfect, and that's very true. The more that you practice, the more you can do! Get to know your machine, each and every part, and in no time at all you'll be ready to start ....SEWING!!

Parts of a sewing machine

Each sewing machine will come with it's own instruction booklet...but most machines have very similar parts. Why not compare this picture to YOUR sewing machine. Try to find each part on yours!

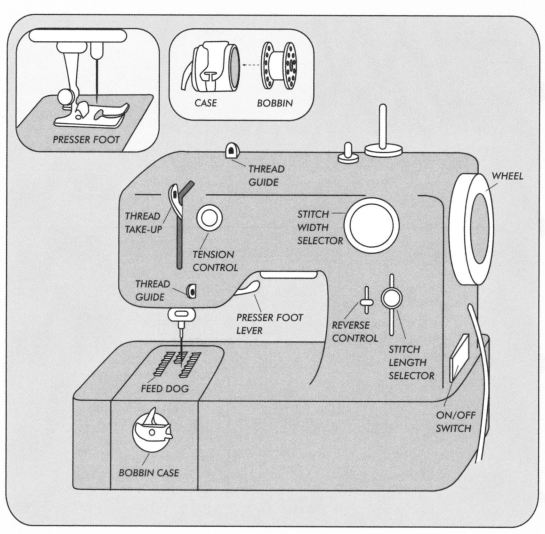

WHEEL — This turns as the machine goes. By turning the wheel **towards** you, you can raise and lower the needle to place it exactly where you want.

ON/OFF SWITCH — This turns the power on and off.

REVERSE CONTROL — Use this lever to sew backwards.

STITCH WIDTH SELECTOR — Adjust this dial to change your straight stitch to a zigzag stitch.

STITCH LENGTH SELECTOR — Adjust this to set the length of your stitch.

TENSION CONTROL — This controls the amount of pressure on your thread as it passes through your machine. You shouldn't normally have to adjust this.

THREAD GUIDES — These guides lead your thread from the spool all the way to the needle.

THREAD TAKE-UP — This lever helps to keep the tension on the thread. We can also look at this to see if our needle is **up** or **down** when we want to stop or start.

BOBBIN CASE — The bobbin case holds the bobbin, and the bobbin holds the bottom thread.

PRESSER FOOT — The presser foot works with the feed dog to hold the fabric and move it through the machine. Presser feet come in different shapes for different jobs.

PRESSER FOOT LEVER — This lever raises and lowers the presser foot. Raise it to insert your fabric. Lower it when ready to sew.

FEED DOG — The feed dog teeth and presser foot work together to move the fabric along. Can you see the teeth?

How to...
Thread your machine

Check the instruction booklet to see where all the thread guides are on your machine.

Follow the path from the spool, through all the thread guides to the needle's eye. Don't miss any out!

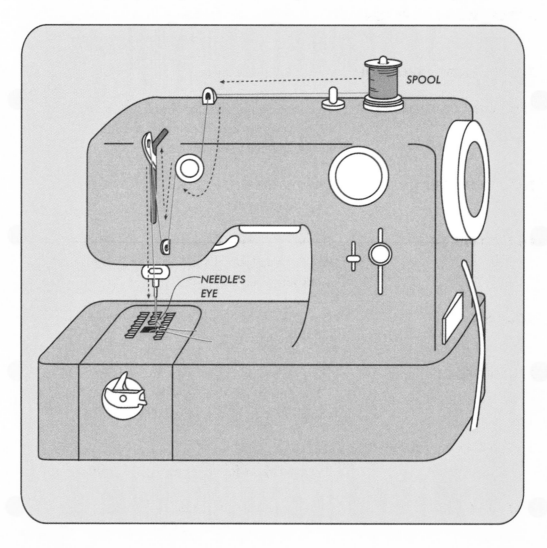

SPOOL

NEEDLE'S EYE

How to...
Fill the bobbin

Sewing machines use two different threads — the top spool and the bottom bobbin. When the machine goes, both threads join together to make a stitch!

STEP 1
Follow the thread guides from the spool to the bobbin winder and wind thread onto your bobbin.

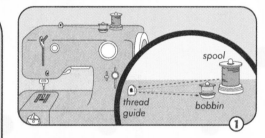

STEP 2
Put the bobbin in the bobbin case...

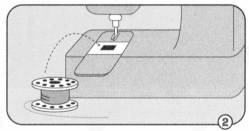

STEP 3
...and then turn the wheel to bring the bobbin thread up through the needle hole.

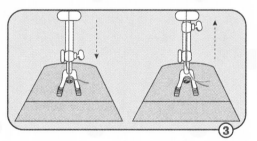

Hands and positioning

It's important that we're sitting comfortably at our sewing machine. Make sure that you can sit up straight with your feet flat on the floor. Can you reach the foot pedal easily?

Make a triangle with your hands, resting your fingertips on the fabric to lightly guide it through. Practice controlling your fabric so that the machine sews exactly where you want it to!

Don't PUSH or PULL the fabric ... just GUIDE it!

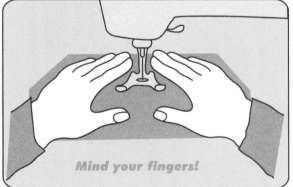

Mind your fingers!

Quiz: Parts of a sewing machine

Can you remember the names of all the parts of a sewing machine? Fill in the quiz below!

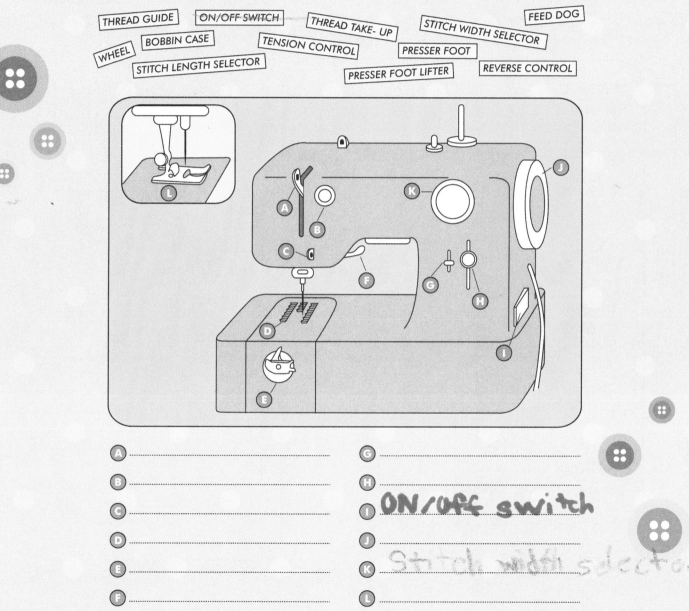

THREAD GUIDE   ON/OFF SWITCH   THREAD TAKE-UP   STITCH WIDTH SELECTOR   FEED DOG

WHEEL   BOBBIN CASE   TENSION CONTROL   PRESSER FOOT

STITCH LENGTH SELECTOR   PRESSER FOOT LIFTER   REVERSE CONTROL

A ....

B ....

C ....

D ....

E ....

F ....

G ....

H ....

I   ON/off switch

J ....

K   Stitch width selector

L ....

How to...
Turn corners

To turn corners, or 'pivot' with a sewing machine, we need to pay close attention to our needle and our presser foot. Imagine your needle is a ballerina's foot! The needle, like the dancer's toe, must stay down as you lift the presser foot, turn the fabric, then drop the presser foot back down.

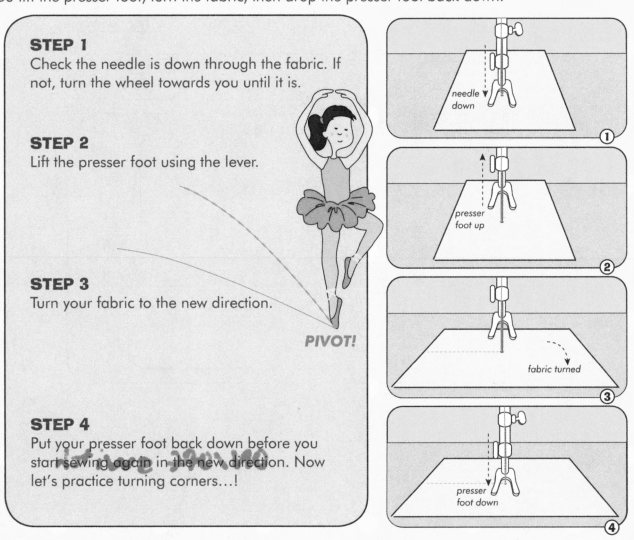

STEP 1
Check the needle is down through the fabric. If not, turn the wheel towards you until it is.

STEP 2
Lift the presser foot using the lever.

STEP 3
Turn your fabric to the new direction.

PIVOT!

STEP 4
Put your presser foot back down before you start sewing again in the new direction. Now let's practice turning corners...!

needle down
①

presser foot up
②

fabric turned
③

presser foot down
④

Practice...
Turning corners

Copy this page, don't tear the book!

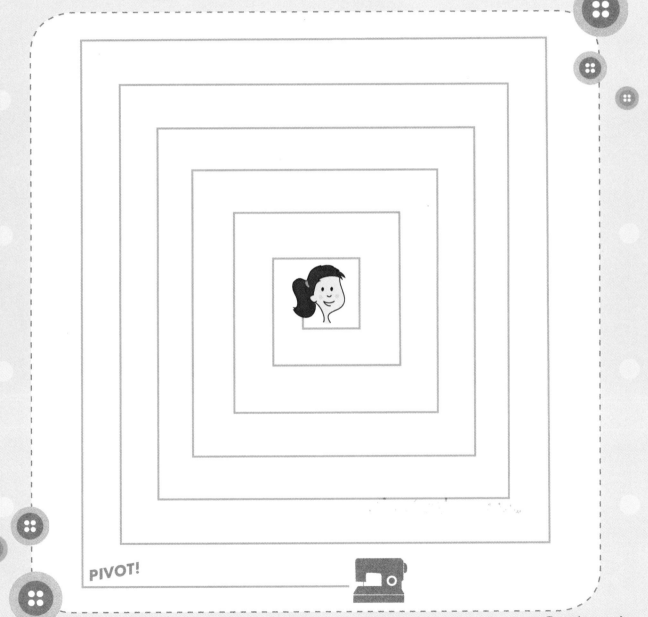

PIVOT!

How to sew...
Lock stitches

When we sew by hand, we always **start** and **finish** with a **DOUBLE STITCH**. It's no different with a sewing machine — we do the same and this is called a **LOCK STITCH**.

STEP 1
Start sewing for a few stitches on your machine.

STEP 2
Use the **reverse** lever to stitch **backwards** to where you started.

STEP 3
Release the **reverse** lever and stitch on as normal.

STEP 4
Stitch all the way to where you need to end then **reverse** for a few stitches. See if you can practice doing lock stitches on your practice pages.

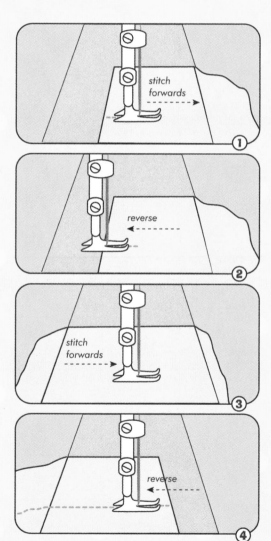

Practice sewing...
Lock stitches

Don't forget to start by going forwards for a few stitches, then reverse to make your lock stitch... the blue dots show you where!

Practice sewing...
Straight lines

Copy this page, don't tear the book!

Practice sewing...
A star shape

Copy this page,
don't tear the book!

Remember to 'pivot' to change direction!

Practice sewing...
Curves

Copy this page, don't tear the book!

Practice sewing...
A heart shape

Copy this page, don't tear the book!

Easy Tote Bag

For a large tote bag, cut two pieces of fabric 35cm x 40cm, and two handles 70cm long.
For a mini tote bag, cut two pieces of fabric 20cm x 25cm, and two handles 50cm long.
For easy handles, use webbing or woven handle tape.

STEP 1

Hem along one short edge of each piece of fabric.

STEP 2

Pin your handles in place, with 5cm at each end inside the bag

STEP 3

Sew a square around the ends of your handles to attach them to the bag. Do this a few times to make it strong!

STEP 4

Now place your fabric right sides together. Pin. Sew from one top side to the other. Now turn your bag the right way out!

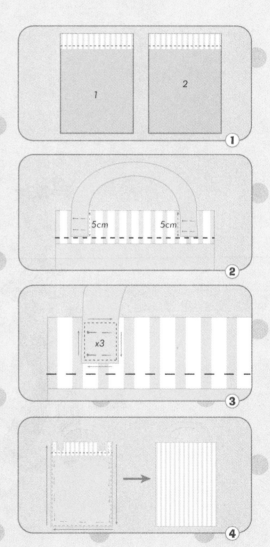

Cool Cushions

What size is the cushion you want to cover? Measure the sides! Then cut your fabric as follows:

For the front of the cushion cover, add 5cm to the size of your cushion on all four edges.
For the back of the cover, cut your fabric 20cm longer than the front square.

STEP 1
Cut out your fabric to size. If your cushion is 50cm x 50cm you can use the measurements in the diagram. Take the longer back piece and cut this in half to make two panels. Sew a hem along one of the long sides of each panel.

STEP 2
If you would like to decorate the front of your cushion, do this now to the front panel **BEFORE** you stitch it.

STEP 3
Lay the front square on the table, decorated side **up**. Position one of the back panels, face down, with the hem facing towards the middle. Lay the second panel on top in the same way. Pin these in place then sew all around the square 2cm in from the edges of the cushion cover.

STEP 4
Now turn your cool cushion cover right sides out and insert your cushion!

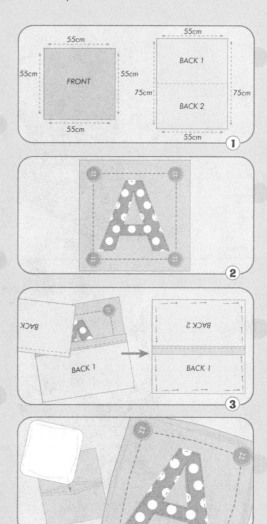

Zip Cases

For a small Cosmetics bag: cut 2 pieces of fabric 24cm x 18cm. Use a 20cm zip.

For a larger Toiletry bag: cut 2 pieces of fabrics 34cm x 28cm. Use a 30cm zip.

STEP 1

Position the zip along the long edge of one fabric piece, with the right side* of the zip facing the right side of the fabric. Sew close to the raw edge.

STEP 2

Sew the other side of the zip to the 2nd piece of fabric in the same way. If you wish to add any ribbon or trim to your zip case, do this now. Open the zip half way, so you can turn it right side out after sewing the case up.

STEP 3

Position the fabric panels right sides together and sew around the sides and base of your bag.

STEP 4

Separate the 2 layers at the lower corners and refold them diagonally, so that the side and base seams are on top of each other. Stitch across at right angles to the seams. Trim the point away and turn the bag right side out.

I-Pod Case

These little cases are so easy and fun to make — why not make lots of presents? They can be used for cash, phones and mp3 players too!

STEP 1
Cut a long rectangle from a piece of fabric and fold it in half. With the wrong side facing you, fold each end over about 2cm/3/4in and pin. Sew a line of Straight Stitch along both ends about 1cm/1/2in away from the folded edge.

STEP 2
Decorate the front of your bag before you sew the rest together, so use stitches, ribbons and appliqué to make it look lovely! Remember to check which way is up for both sides of the bag.

STEP 3
Now fold the fabric in half with the right sides together. Pin the edges, then Backstitch along each side 1cm/3/4in from the edge. Turn bag right sides out.

STEP 4
Cut 2 pieces of ribbon, each about 3 times the width of your bag. Attach a safety pin to the end of 1 piece of ribbon and push it through from 1 folded edge to the other. Tie the ribbon ends together with a knot. Starting at the opposite side of the bag, do the same again with the second ribbon.

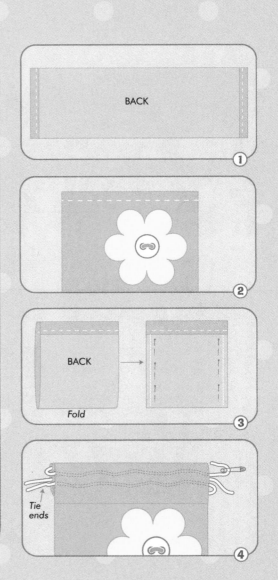

Draughty Dog

This doggy pal is a great way to block chilly draughts from coming under your window or door! You can even use scrap fabric or scrunched up newspaper to fill him, so he's kind to the environment too! What will you call your doggy friend?

STEP 1

Cut a strip of fabric 25cm/10in wide, and as long as you want your dog to be. Fold your fabric strip so that the right side is on the inside and the two long sides are touching. Use the dog's head pattern (p.75) at one end of your strip to cut the curved end for his head!

STEP 2

Sew about 1cm/1/2in in from the edge from the tail to the end of the nose. Remember to begin and end with a double stitch. Leave the tail end open so that you can turn it right side out and stuff it.

STEP 3

Now turn your dog tube right side out. Poke a pencil into it from the inside so that the nose part is nice and pointy! Stuff your dog with used paper or even cut up carrier bags. Stuff your dog with toy filling, or old fabric or scrunched up newspaper.

STEP 4

Now cut the eyes, nose, ears and tail from the felt using the patterns provided. Sew these on to give your dog his personality. Now he's ready to be your new pet.

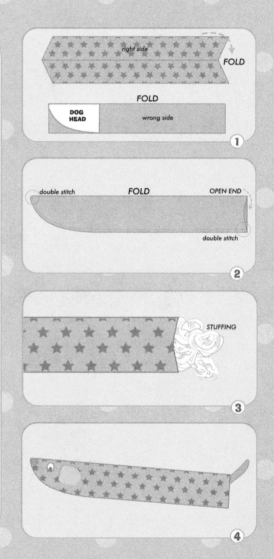

Simple Skirt

Fabric: Measure around the widest part of your hips and add 10cm. This will be the width of your fabric. If you would like your skirt to be fuller, with more gathers, increase this. Measure the desired length of the skirt and add 6cm for the casing and hem allowance.

STEP 1
Start by zig zag stitching around all the raw edges of your fabric to neaten. Fold the fabric in half widthways, right sides together. Machine stitch a 1cm side seam from top to bottom.

STEP 2
To make a casing for the elastic waist, pin a 4cm hem and sew all the way around, leaving a 3cm gap at the centre back. This is where you will thread the elastic through.

STEP 3
Cut a piece of elastic 2cm shorter than your waist measurement. Secure one end with a safety pin, and use another safety pin to feed it through the casing, gathering the skirt as you go. Hold end together with a safety pin and try on to fit. Once happy with the tightness of your waistband, sew the ends of the elastic together on the machine.

STEP 4
Now pin and sew the hem!

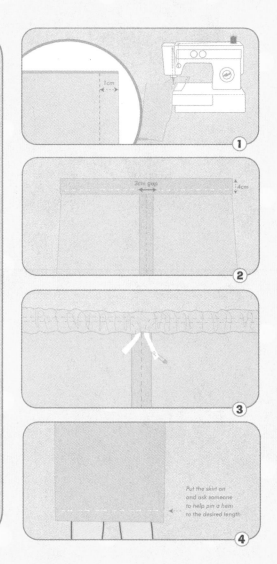

Ice cream & Cupcake Pattern

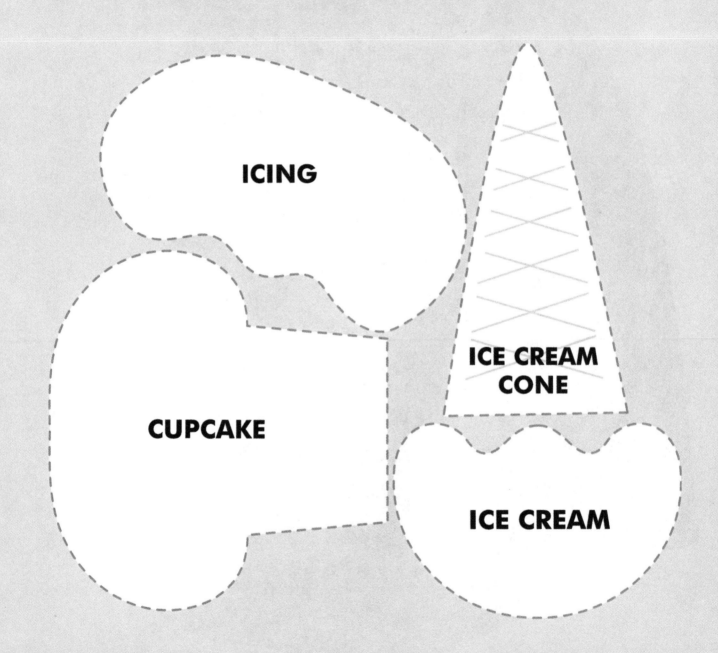

ICING

ICE CREAM CONE

CUPCAKE

ICE CREAM

Draughty Dog Patterns

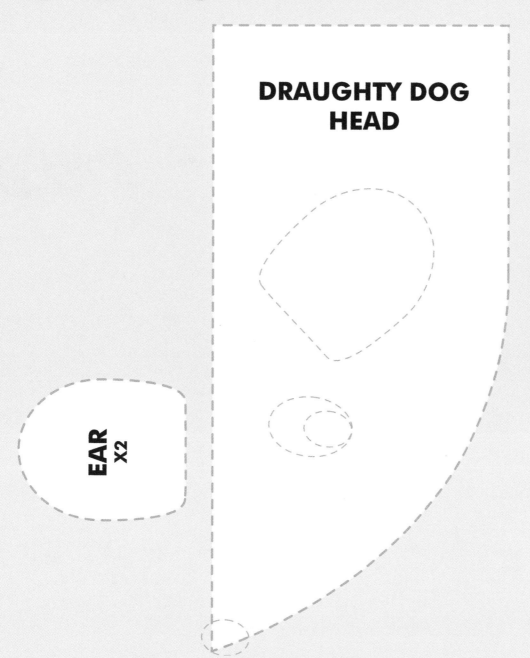

DRAUGHTY DOG
HEAD

EAR
X2

Learn to Sew: Kids

I hope you've had tons of fun learning to sew...why not add to your skills with my other books:

Learn To Sew: Kids
My First Hand Sewing Book

The perfect introduction to sewing for beginners. Follow Daisy Doublestitch and Billy Bobbin as they show you how to sew by hand and learn lots of easy stitches and sewing skills. Make super cool projects like Cupcake Pincushions, Crazy Creatures, Birdy Garlands, lovely Love Hearts and more!

Learn To Sew: Kids
More Hand Sewing Fun!

Add to your hand sewing skills with more great stitches and skills and make even more cool projects Kitten Slippers, Cute Cushions, Strawberry Purses, Tissue Monsters, Gingerbread men and more!

Learn To Sew: Kids
My First Sewing Machine

Get started with your first sewing machine with easy to follow illustrations and instructions! Learn all the parts of a machine and what they do, how to thread your machine and wind your bobbin, how to start and stop sewing, turn corners...AND make your first easy projects — cushions, bags, zip cases, skirts, i-pod cases and more! Sew much fun!